ZOODLES

Bernard Most

Harcourt Brace & Company

San Diego · New York · London

Requests for permission to make copies of any part of
the work should be mailed to: Permissions Department,
Harcourt Brace & Company, 6277 Sea Harbor Drive, Orlando, Florida 32887-6777.

Library of Congress Cataloging-in-Publication Data
Most, Bernard.
Zoodles/by Bernard Most.
p.   cm.
Summary: A collection of riddles about fanciful combination animals, including
"What do you call a kangaroo that wakes you up every day? A kangarooster."
ISBN 0-15-299969-8
1. Riddles, Juvenile. 2. Animals — Juvenile humor.
[1. Riddles. 2. Animals — Wit and humor.] I. title.
PN6371.5.M64   1992
818'.5402 — dc20   91-33490

B C D E F

Printed in Singapore

The illustrations in this book were done in Pantone markers
on Bainbridge board 172, hot-press finish.
The display type and text type were set in Antique Olive
by Thompson Type, San Diego, California.
Color separations were made by Bright Arts, Ltd., Singapore.
Production supervision by Warren Wallerstein and Ginger Boyer
Designed by Camilla Filancia

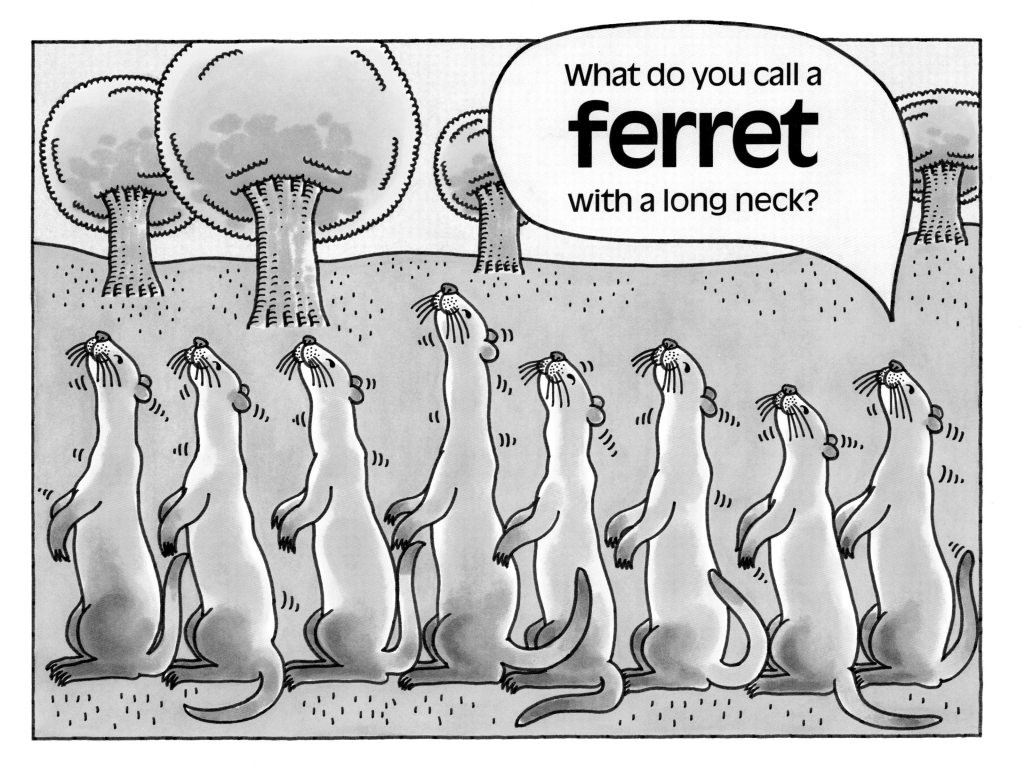

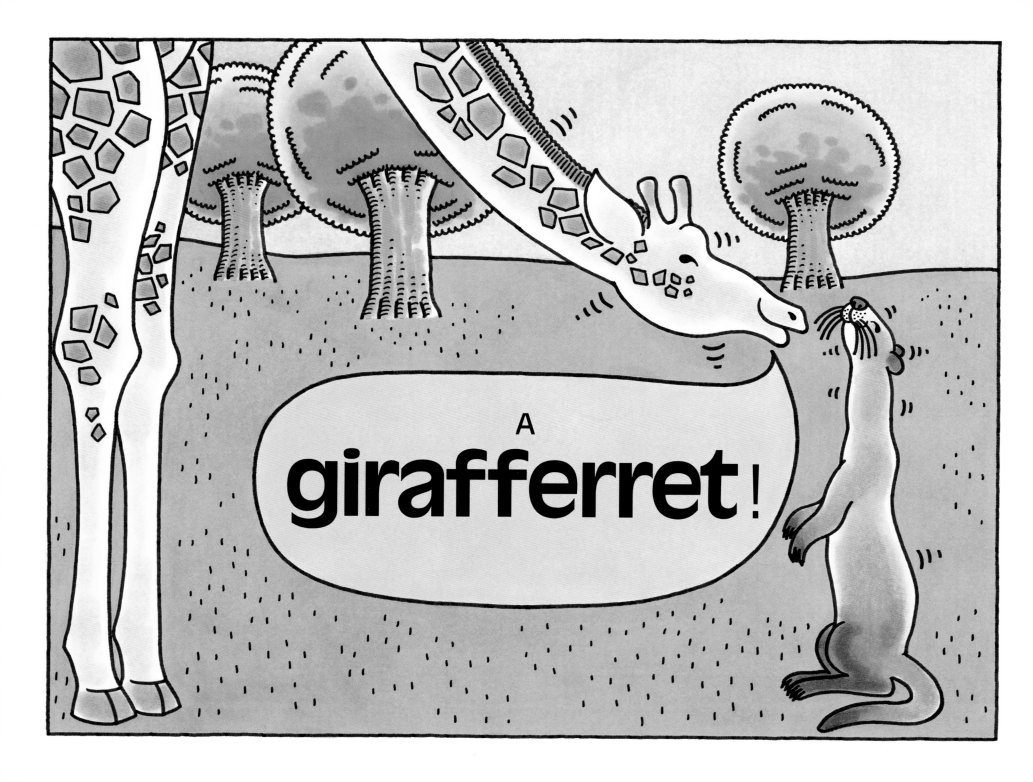

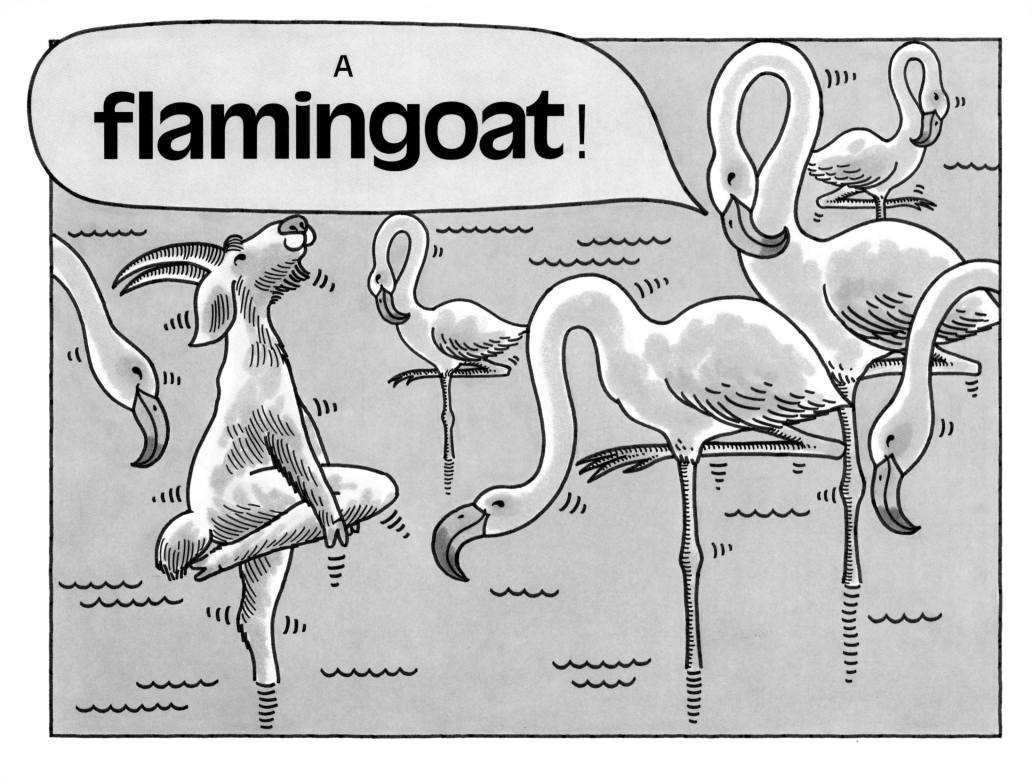

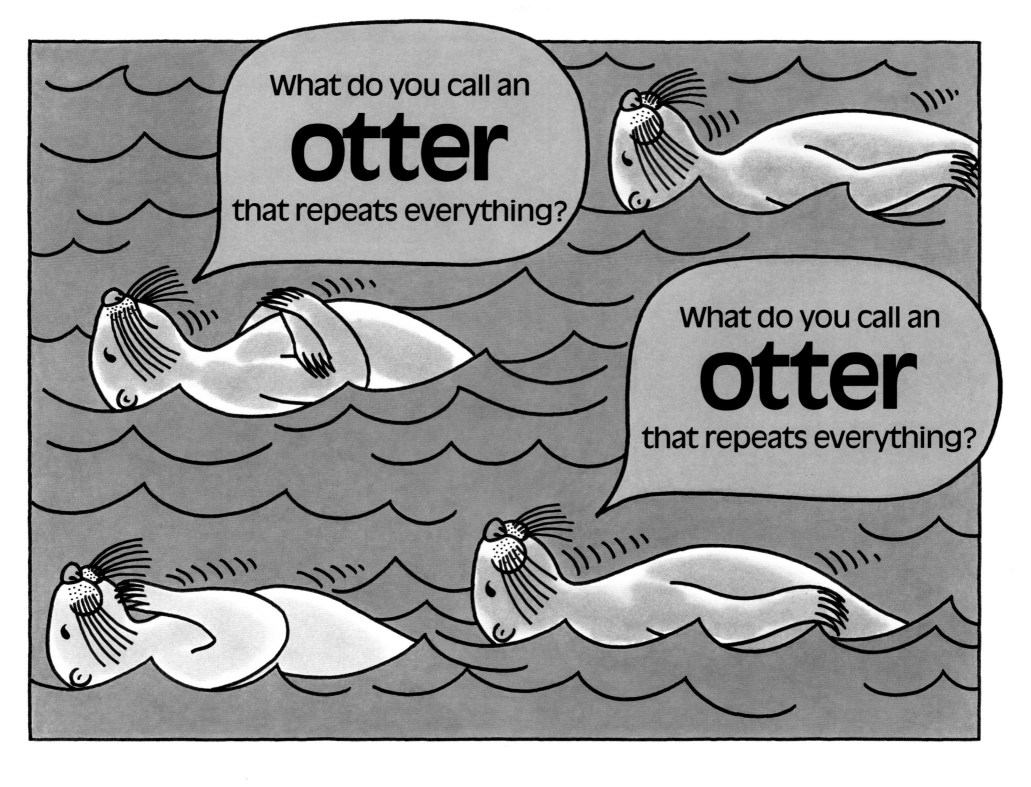

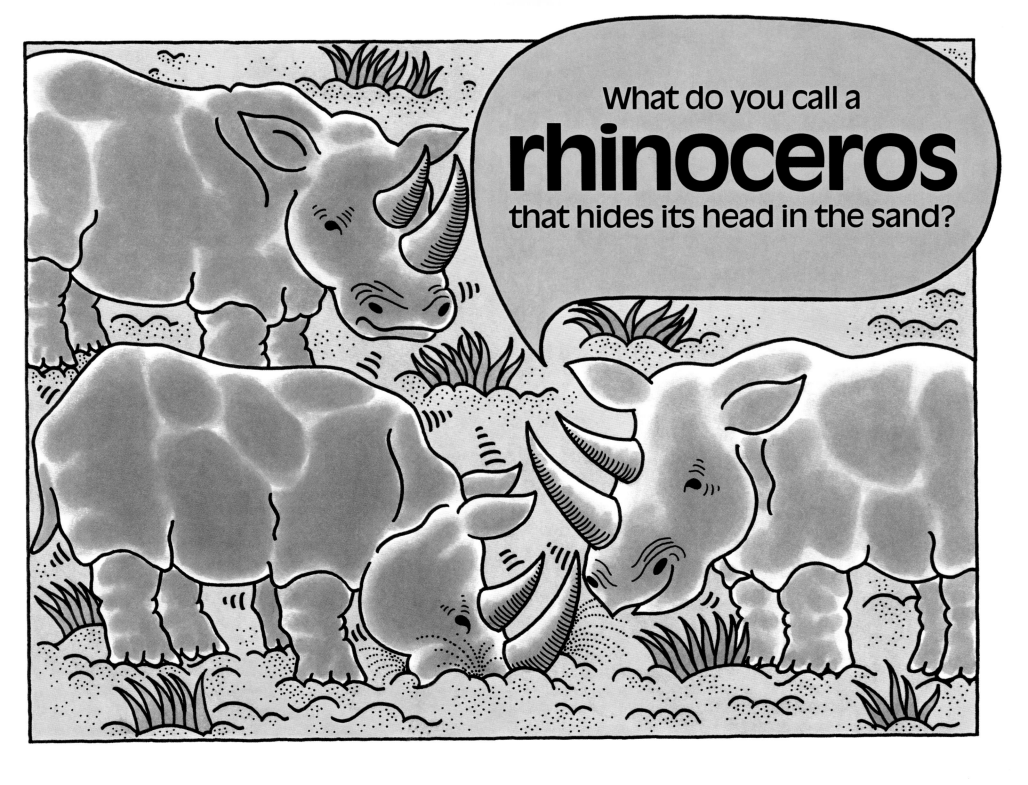